Being a
Writer™
SECOND EDITION

First edition published 2007. Second edition 2014.

Being a Writer is a trademark of Center for the Collaborative Classroom.

Center for the Collaborative Classroom wishes to thank the following authors, agents, and publishers for their permission to reprint materials included in this program. Every effort has been made to trace the ownership of copyrighted material and to make full acknowledgment of its use. If errors or omissions have occurred, they will be corrected in subsequent printings, provided that notification is submitted in writing to the publisher.

Excerpt from *Miss Tizzy* by Libba Moore Gray. Text copyright © 1993 by Libba Moore Gray. Reprinted with the permission of Simon & Schuster Books for Young Readers, an imprint of Simon & Schuster Children's Publishing Division. Excerpts from *HONK! The Story of a Prima Swanerina* by Pamela Duncan Edwards. Text copyright © 1998 by Pamela Duncan Edwards. Reprinted by permission of Disney • Hyperion Books, an imprint of Disney Books Group, LLC. All rights reserved. "Q&A with Isobel Springett: The Photographer of *Kate & Pippin*," published by Center for the Collaborative Classroom, is adapted from text provided by Isobel Springett. Copyright © 2013 by Isobel Springett. "Which Is Stronger?" adapted from "Corrugated Paper" from *Super Science Experiments* by Muriel Mandell. Copyright © 2005. Published by Sterling Publishing Co., Inc. Excerpt from *Polar Animals* (*Who Lives Here?* series), written by Deborah Hodge and illustrated by Pat Stephens, is used by permission of Kids Can Press Ltd., Toronto. Text copyright © 2008 by Deborah Hodge. Illustrations copyright © 2008 by Pat Stephens. "Sea Mammals" excerpt from *Polar Lands* by Margaret Hynes. Copyright © 2005 by Kingfisher Publications Plc. Reprinted by permission of Kingfisher Publications Plc., an imprint of Houghton Mifflin Company. All rights reserved. Whale photo: Getty Images, Inc. copyright © 1999–2008 by Getty Images, Inc. All rights reserved. All other photos: Bryan and Cherry Alexander Photography. Used by permission of the photographer. Copyright © 2002–2007 by Nature Picture Library/Doc White. All rights reserved. "Modern Life" excerpt from *Polar Lands* by Margaret Hynes. Copyright © 2005 by Kingfisher Publications Plc. Reprinted by permission of Kingfisher Publications Plc., an imprint of Houghton Mifflin Company. All rights reserved. Images © B&C Alexander/Arcticphoto. Excerpt from *First Year Letters* text copyright © 2003 by Julie Danneberg. Illustrations copyright © 2003 by Judy Love. Used with permission by Charlesbridge Publishing, Inc. 85 Main Street, Watertown, MA 02472. 617-926-0329. www. charlesbridge.com. All rights reserved. "Tree House" and "Boa Constrictor" from *Where the Sidewalk Ends*. Copyright © 2004 by Evil Eye Music, Inc. Reprinted with permission from the estate of Shel Silverstein and HarperCollins Children's Books. Used by permission of HarperCollins Publishers. "The Coyote" and "The Tiger" from *Mammalabilia* by Douglas Florian. Copyright © 2000 by Douglas Florian. Reprinted by permission of Houghton Mifflin Harcourt Publishing Company. All rights reserved. "Knoxville, Tennessee" from *Black Feeling, Black Talk, Black Judgment* by Nikki Giovanni. Copyright © 1968, 1970 by Nikki Giovanni. Reprinted by permission of HarperCollins Publishers. "Lettuce"/"Lechuga" text copyright © 1997 by Alma Flor Ada; English translation copyright © 1997 by Rosa Zubizarreta, from *Gathering the Sun: An Alphabet in Spanish and English*. Used by permission of HarperCollins Publishers. "Peaches"/"Duraznos" text copyright © 1997 by Alma Flor Ada; English translation copyright © 1997 by Rosa Zubizarreta, from *Gathering the Sun: An Alphabet in Spanish and English*. Used by permission of HarperCollins Publishers. "My Baby Brother" from *Fathers, Mothers, Sisters, Brothers: A Collection of Family Poems* by Mary Ann Hoberman; illustrated by Marylin Hafner. Text copyright © 1959, 1991 by Mary Ann Hoberman; illustrations copyright © 1991 by Marylin Hafner. By permission of Little, Brown and Company and the Gina Maccoby Literary Agency. All rights reserved. "Wind Song" from *I Feel the Same Way* by Lilian Moore. Copyright © 1966, 1967 Lilian Moore. All rights renewed and reserved. Used by permission of Marian Reiner. "Weather" from *Always Wondering: Some Favorite Poems of Aileen Fisher*. Copyright © 1991 Aileen Fisher. Used by permission of Marian Reiner on behalf of the Boulder Public Library Foundation, Inc. "Fish" from *The Llama Who Had No Pajama: 100 Favorite Poems* by Mary Ann Hoberman. Text copyright © 1959 and renewed 1987 by Mary Ann Hoberman. Reprinted by permission of Houghton Mifflin Harcourt Publishing Company and the Gina Maccoby Literary Agency. All rights reserved. "Clouds" by Christina G. Rossetti from *Sing a Song of Popcorn*. Copyright © 1988, selected by Beatrice Schenk de Regniers, Eva Moore, Mary Michaels White, and Jan Carr, and published by Scholastic, Inc. "Rain Poem" by Elizabeth Coatsworth. Used by permission of The Marsh Agency Ltd on behalf of the estate of Elizabeth Coatsworth. All rights reserved. "Buses" by Maxine Kumin from *No One Writes a Letter to a Snail*. Copyright © 1962 Maxine Kumin. Used by permission of The Anderson Literary Agency Inc. Excerpts from *Should We Have Pets?* by Sylvia Lollis. Copyright © 2003 Mondo Publishing. Used by permission.

Cover illustration by Michael Wertz

Center for the Collaborative Classroom
1001 Marina Village Parkway, Suite 110
Alameda, CA 94501
(800) 666-7270; fax: (510) 464-3670
collaborativeclassroom.org

ISBN 978-1-61003-254-4

Printed in the United States of America

17 18 19 20 21 22 BNG 26 25 24 23 22 21 20 19

Being a Writer™

SECOND EDITION

from *Miss Tizzy*

by Libba Moore Gray

On Fridays, Miss Tizzy opened her trunk and they all played dress up. There were hats with feathers and hats with bows. There were baseball caps and straw hats with bright, red bands. Everyone wore a hat. Miss Tizzy put on a lace shawl and served pink lemonade in her best china cups. The children loved it.

from *HONK! The Story of a Prima Swanerina*
by Pamela Duncan Edwards

"Oh, no! She's at it again!" honked the goose.

"Clear a landing space!" quacked the duck.

"Guard your lily pads!" croaked the frogs.

"Watch out! Here she comes."

Mimi flew down in a perfect ballet pose.

SPLASH!

"Mimi!" cried her friends. "Stop doing that! You're driving us crazy!"

But Mimi wasn't listening. She was whirling around the pond *en pointe*.

Excerpt

from *HONK! The Story of a Prima Swanerina*
by Pamela Duncan Edwards

In winter, a new production came to the Opera House. Mimi watched with interest.

"How pretty!" she exclaimed. "How glistening! How FEATHERY! How AMAZING!"

"What's up?" asked a pigeon.

"They're all pretending to be me!" cried Mimi in delight. "They must have noticed me practicing."

"Probably," said the pigeon. "We certainly have!"

Q&A with Isobel Springett: The Photographer of *Kate & Pippin*

Q: Were you surprised that Kate and Pippin became such good friends?

A: I was quite surprised when Kate and Pippin became friends. It wasn't my intention when I started caring for Pippin. I had only hoped to keep the fawn warm until I decided what to do next.

Q: Where do Kate and Pippin live?

A: Kate and Pippin live on a large acreage (amount of land) on Vancouver Island, Canada. There are lots of fields and streams, with forests too. There is a big mountain nearby with lots of snow in the winter. It is a deer's heaven!

Q: How often does Pippin visit Kate?

A: Pippin visits almost every day. She comes by more often in the summer and loves to nap with Kate in the shade of our cherry tree. In the winter, she stays in the woods with the other deer and visits in the evenings for treats.

(continues)

Q&A with Isobel Springett: The Photographer of *Kate & Pippin* (continued)

Q: What kinds of things do Kate and Pippin like to do together?

A: Kate and Pippin sometimes go for walks. Other times, they just like to hang out together on the lawn. Now and then, they play and romp but not as much as when Pippin was young. They enjoy each other's company even if they're just sleeping.

Q: Was there ever a time when Kate and Pippin didn't get along? What happened?

A: Kate and Pippin have never had a fight. They always get along.

Q: Did Pippin ever have any fawns of her own?

A: Pippin has given birth to five fawns of her own. The first one didn't survive, but the next four were all healthy and happy.

(continues)

Q&A with Isobel Springett: The Photographer of *Kate & Pippin* (continued)

Q: How do you make sure that Pippin doesn't start thinking of herself as a pet?

A: Pippin knows that she's a deer. She was raised by Kate, but she has spent most of her life with her wild herd. Even if we moved away, she would be just fine. It might be a bit sad for her at first, but she would adjust. Kate would probably miss her though.

Q: Now that Pippin is grown, do you think she thinks of Kate as her mother or her friend? Why?

A: Animals don't really think about parents and friends like humans do. Animals only respond to situations as they occur. That is why Pippin and Kate have no trouble with their relationship. Even though Pippin knows where she belongs, she still accepts Kate as her friend. Humans sometimes have trouble with this concept. I think this is why Kate and Pippin inspire people the way they do. It doesn't matter where you're

(continues)

from, or what you look like—you can become friends with anyone.

Q: What else would you like to share with us about Kate and Pippin?

A: Kate is almost 11 years old. That's pretty old for a Great Dane. She only eats raw food and gets lots of exercise. She weighs 112 pounds and is almost 3 feet tall. Kate was five months old when I got her. She was so scared then, but now she is very friendly and loves kids. Kate is very agile, obedient, and loves to go for rides in the car. Her favorite thing to do is eat.

Pippin is a Coastal Black-tailed deer. She was so tiny when we found her that our cat, Henry, weighed more than her. Pippin is almost five years old. She was born in June 2008. Pippin loves to nibble on corn and fruit. Her favorite things to eat are cherry leaves.

Which Is Stronger?

Which is stronger: a flat piece of paper or a folded piece of paper? Try this experiment to find out.

What You Need:

- 2 sheets of paper
- 2 cans that are the same size
- Small object that won't break, such as an eraser or a marker

What You Do:

1. Fold one sheet of paper "accordion" style by making a ½" fold along the long edge of the paper, turning the sheet over and making another fold the same width as the first fold, and continuing to fold back and forth until the entire sheet is folded. Set this folded piece of paper aside.

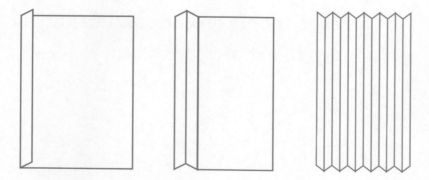

(continues)

"Which Is Stronger?" adapted from "Corrugated Paper" from *Super Science Experiments* by Muriel Mandell. Copyright © 2005. Published by Sterling Publishing Co., Inc.

Which Is Stronger? *(continued)*

2. Put the two cans in front of you, about 5" apart. Place the unfolded sheet of paper on top to make a bridge.

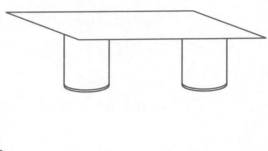

3. Predict, or guess, what will happen when you put your object on the bridge. Will the object cause the bridge to fall?

4. After you make your prediction, place your object on the bridge to see what happens.

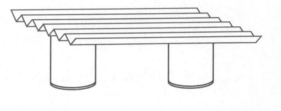

5. Do the same experiment with the folded piece of paper. Remember, predict what you think will happen when you put your object on the folded paper, and then try it.

6. What did you find out? Write about your thinking.

"Which Is Stronger?" adapted from "Corrugated Paper" from *Super Science Experiments* by Muriel Mandell. Copyright © 2005. Published by Sterling Publishing Co., Inc.

Suck It Up!

Which is more absorbent: a sheet of paper or a paper towel? Try this experiment to find out.

What You Need:

- 2 paper towels
- 2 sheets of writing paper
- Marker
- Squeeze bottle or jar with a dropper
- Water

What You Do:

1. On a paper towel, drop a little water. Talk about what happens.

2. Drop the same amount of water onto one of the sheets of writing paper. Talk about what happens.

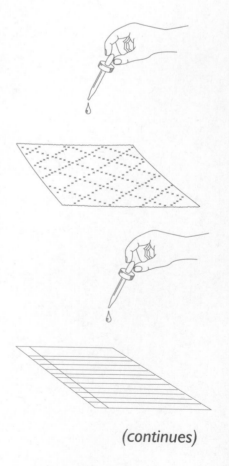

(continues)

Suck It Up! *(continued)*

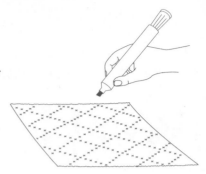

3. On the other paper towel, draw a happy face using a marker. Talk about what you notice.

4. On the other sheet of writing paper, draw a happy face using a marker. Talk about what you notice.

5. What did you find out? Write about your thinking.

Excerpt from *Polar Animals*
by Deborah Hodge, illustrated by Pat Stephens

What Is a Polar Region?

A polar region is a very cold place. For most of the year, thick snow and ice cover the ground. Oceans freeze and fierce winds blow. The Arctic and Antarctic are polar regions.

The Arctic is home to many amazing creatures. Like all polar animals, their bodies are built for living in the cold.

4

(continues)

Brr! Antarctica is the coldest place on Earth. Whales, seals and seabirds are the only large animals that can live here.

Some polar animals live on pack ice — large areas of sea ice floating in the ocean.

Arctic land is called tundra. Caribou and other animals gobble up plants that grow here in the short summer.

5

Excerpt from *Polar Lands*
by Margaret Hynes

24 Sea mammals

The polar oceans are home to whales, seals, sea lions, and walrus. These mammals have blubber to keep them warm and streamlined bodies that help them easily move through the water.

Making a splash
Whales, such as this humpback whale, swim in the icy polar waters. They leap up into the air and fall back into the water with a splash. This is called breaching.

(continues)

Excerpt from *Polar Lands* (continued)

Changing coats

(25)

Harp seals are born with fluffy white coats. The mothers take care of their babies for about two weeks, and then the pups grow gray adult coats and must look after themselves.

Tusk tools

Walrus drag themselves out of the water using their tusks as levers. They also use their tusks to dislodge shellfish on the seabed.

Excerpt from *Polar Lands*
by Margaret Hynes

36 Modern life

Improvements in transportation, construction, food, and clothing have brought a modern way of life to the Arctic. Most people now live in small towns and work in modern industries.

Arctic towns

Arctic towns are like other small towns, except that water has to be delivered by truck. The water would freeze if it was distributed through pipes.

People carrier

The people living in polar lands no longer rely on animals for transportation. Today, they travel on snowmobiles— motorized sleds.

(continues)

Excerpt from *Polar Lands* (continued)

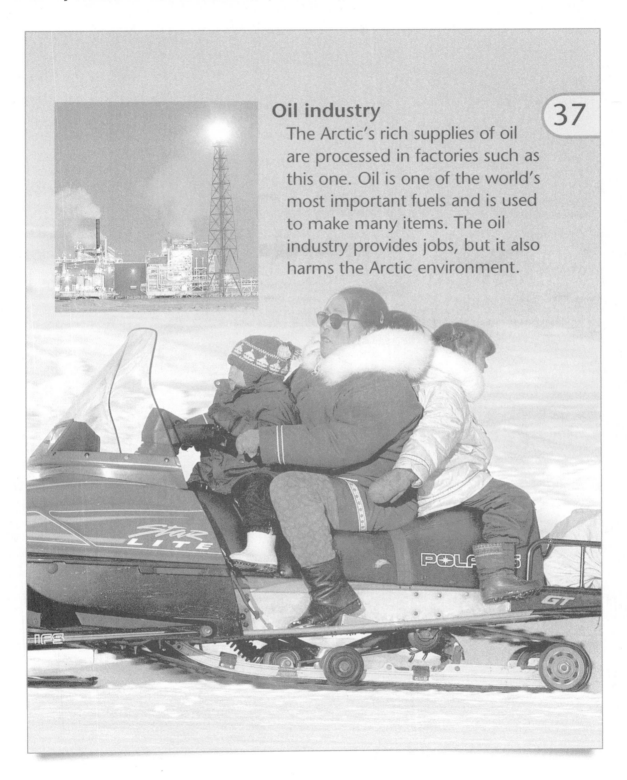

Oil industry

37

The Arctic's rich supplies of oil are processed in factories such as this one. Oil is one of the world's most important fuels and is used to make many items. The oil industry provides jobs, but it also harms the Arctic environment.

Excerpt from *First Year Letters*

by Julie Danneberg, illustrated by Judy Love

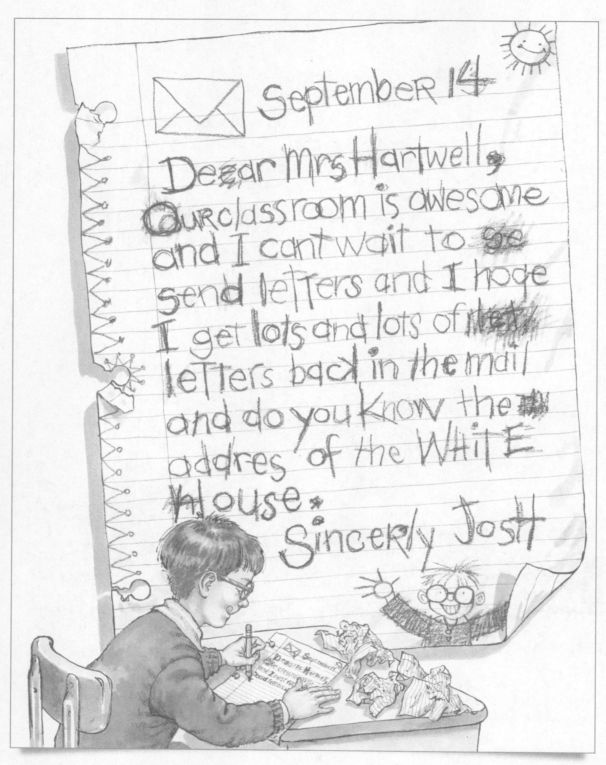

Addressing an Envelope

Joy Jensen

12 Evergreen Way

Woodstock, Vermont 05091

Omar Robinson

625 King Street, Apt. 6

Freehold, New Jersey 07728

Tree House

by Shel Silverstein

A tree house, a free house,
A secret you and me house,
A high up in the leafy branches
Cozy as can be house.

A street house, a neat house,
Be sure and wipe your feet house
Is not my kind of house at all—
Let's go live in a tree house.

Boa Constrictor

by Shel Silverstein

Oh, I'm being eaten
By a boa constrictor,
A boa constrictor,
A boa constrictor,
I'm being eaten by a boa constrictor,
And I don't like it—one bit.
Well, what do you know?
It's nibblin' my toe.
Oh, gee,
It's up to my knee.
Oh my,
It's up to my thigh.
Oh, fiddle,
It's up to my middle.
Oh, heck,
It's up to my neck.
Oh, dread,
It's upmmmmmmmmmmmfffffffffff . . .

The Coyote
by Douglas Florian

I prowl.

I growl.

My howl

Is throaty.

I love

A vowel,

For I am coyo$^{o^{o^o}o}$ote.

Poem

The Tiger
by Douglas Florian

I am a cat—come hear me purrrr.
I've many stripes upon my furrrr.
I speed through forests like a blurrrr.
I hunt at night—I am tigerrrr.

Knoxville, Tennessee

by Nikki Giovanni

I always like summer
best
you can eat fresh corn
from daddy's garden
and okra
and greens
and cabbage
and lots of
barbecue
and buttermilk
and homemade ice-cream
at the church picnic

and listen to
gospel music
outside
at the church
homecoming
and go to the mountains with
your grandmother
and go barefooted
and be warm
all the time
not only when you go to bed
and sleep

"Knoxville, Tennessee" from *Black Feeling, Black Talk, Black Judgment* by Nikki Giovanni. Copyright © 1968, 1970 by Nikki Giovanni. Reprinted by permission of HarperCollins Publishers.

Poem

Lettuce

by Alma Flor Ada, English translation by Rosa Zubizarreta

Small, curly,
fresh and wrinkled
heads of bright
green lettuce.

Empty boxes
wait for us
to bend our backs
and fill them up.

Lechuga

Cabecitas rizadas
llenas de arrugas
frescas, lozanas,
verdes lechugas.

Cajas y cajas
vacías esperan
que doblen las espaldas
quienes las llenan.

Poem

Peaches

by Alma Flor Ada, English translation by Rosa Zubizarreta

Juicy, golden peaches,
honey-sweet,
like a gentle caress
in the palm of my hand.

Duraznos

Duraznos jugosos,
almibarados, dorados,
como una caricia suave
en la palma de la mano.

My Baby Brother
by Mary Ann Hoberman

My baby brother's beautiful,
So perfect and so tiny.
His skin is soft and velvet brown;
His eyes are dark and shiny.

His hair is black and curled up tight;
His two new teeth are sharp and white.
I like it when he chews his toes;
And when he laughs, his dimple shows.

Poem

Wind Song
by Lilian Moore

When the wind blows
the quiet things speak.
Some whisper, some clang,
Some creak.

Grasses swish.
Treetops sigh.
Flags slap
and snap at the sky.
Wires on poles
whistle and hum.
Ashcans roll.
Windows drum.

When the wind goes—
suddenly
then,
the quiet things
are quiet again.

Weather
by Aileen Fisher

Weather is full
of the nicest sounds:
it sings
and rustles
and pings
and pounds
and hums
and tinkles
and strums
and twangs
and whishes
and sprinkles
and splishes
and bangs
and mumbles
and grumbles
and rumbles
and flashes
and CRASHES.

"Weather" from *Always Wondering: Some Favorite Poems of Aileen Fisher*. Copyright © 1991 Aileen Fisher.
Used by permission of Marian Reiner on behalf of the Boulder Public Library Foundation, Inc.

Poem

Fish
by Mary Ann Hoberman

Look at them flit
Lickety-split
Wiggling
Swiggling
Swerving
Curving
Hurrying
Scurrying
Chasing
Racing
Whizzing
Whisking
Flying
Frisking
Tearing around
With a leap and a bound
But none of them making the tiniest
                              tiniest
                                 tiniest
                                    tiniest
                                       sound.

Clouds

by Christina G. Rossetti

White sheep, white sheep
On a blue hill,
When the wind stops
You all stand still.
When the wind blows
You walk away slow.
White sheep, white sheep,
Where do you go?

"Clouds" by Christina G. Rossetti from *Sing a Song of Popcorn*. Copyright © 1988, selected by Beatrice Schenk de Regniers, Eva Moore, Mary Michaels White, and Jan Carr, and published by Scholastic, Inc.

Rain Poem

by Elizabeth Coatsworth

The rain was like a little mouse,
quiet, small and gray.
It pattered all around the house
and then it went away.

It did not come, I understand,
indoors at all, until
it found an open window and
left tracks across the sill.

Buses

by Maxine Kumin

Fat and cross, the city buses,
sometimes late and sometimes early,
grunt like hippopotamuses
in the traffic's hurly-burly.

Huffy hippos, nose to tail,
lined up on the river banks,
blink along the narrow trail,
nudging one another's flanks.

Excerpt from *Should We Have Pets?*

by Sylvia Lollis, with Joyce Hogan and her second-grade class

An Argument for Pets

Good for the Animals

"Have you ever seen a dirty, homeless animal on the street? Well, we have, and that's why we think people should own pets— because it's good for animals."

—AMANDA ABEL AND ELIZABETH DUNAWAY

© P. Royer/ Robertstock

Animals need food, water, and a place to live. Pet owners give their animals these things. Too many animals starve to death or die because they don't have a home.

(continues)

Excerpt from *Should We Have Pets?* (continued)

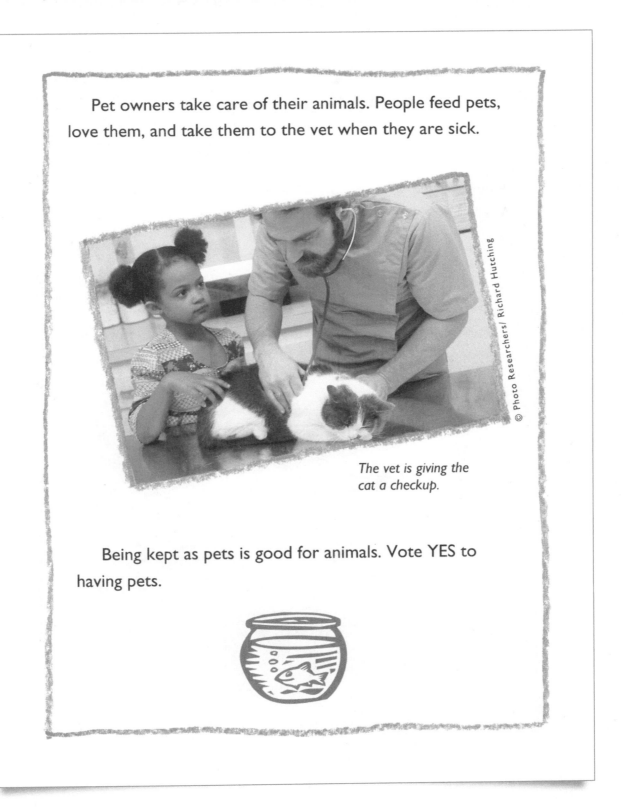

Pet owners take care of their animals. People feed pets, love them, and take them to the vet when they are sick.

© Photo Researchers/ Richard Hutching

The vet is giving the cat a checkup.

Being kept as pets is good for animals. Vote YES to having pets.

Excerpt from *Should We Have Pets?*

by Sylvia Lollis, with Joyce Hogan and her second-grade class

An Argument Against Pets

Pets Cost Too Much

"Pet owners spend a lot of money on food for their animals, but many Americans go hungry."

—BreAunna Gladmon

Sometimes it seems like people care more about animals than people. Some Americans go hungry while most pets are fed fancy, expensive food.

These people are poor and hungry. They have to beg for food.

© Zephyr Pictures/ Camerique Inc./ Robertstock

(continues)

Excerpt from *Should We Have Pets?* (continued)

Most pet owners buy collars, brushes, dishes, leashes, toys, and cages for their pets, too. When a pet gets sick, the owner must pay for the vet and medicine.

This pet store sells expensive things people can buy for their pets.

I think the money pet owners spend on their animals should go to helping people instead. Vote NO to owning pets.

Excerpt from *Should We Have Pets?*

by Sylvia Lollis, with Joyce Hogan and her second-grade class

An Argument for Pets

We Can Learn From Pets

"Our pets have taught us a lot."

—BLANE WILLIAMSON AND ORIN FUSSELL

© ScienceSource.com

Owning a pet is hard work. A pet owner must remember to feed and clean the animal and to bring it to the vet for checkups. Owning a pet teaches a person responsibility, which is an important quality.

(continues)

Excerpt from *Should We Have Pets?* *(continued)*

a mother hamster and babies

© Animals Animals/ Maier, Robert

Having a pet is also educational. Pet owners learn what different animals eat, when they sleep, and how they act. They might even get to see their pet have babies. Owning a pet is a science lesson every day.

Taking care of a pet teaches responsibility and it's educational. We vote YES to owning pets.

Excerpt from *Should We Have Pets?*

by Sylvia Lollis, with Joyce Hogan and her second-grade class

An Argument Against Pets

Animals Should Be Free

"Pet birds have a small space to walk in but not enough room to fly. Some birds get so bored, they pull their own feathers out."

—ROSHANDA HARRIS AND FRANKLIN SHERMAN

© Shutterstock.com/ WilleeCole

We think animals should be free. Animals kept as pets aren't free. It's cruel to keep dogs, cats, birds, fish, rabbits, or any other animals indoors, in cages, or away from their natural habitats.

(continues)

Excerpt from *Should We Have Pets?* (continued)

Most dogs and cats are kept indoors. Most wild dogs roam in packs, and pet dogs would act this way, too, if they were free. Cats are natural hunters that prowl around hunting when given the chance.

Birds are meant to fly, but most pet birds are kept in tiny cages. Fish should be free to swim in ponds, lakes, or oceans, but most pet fish are kept in small bowls or tanks. Living in a cage or bowl your whole life would be very lonely.

© iStockphoto.com/ mehmettoriak

Animals should be free, not kept as pets. We vote NO to owning pets.

Word Bank

A

above	all	animal	around
across	almost	another	as
add	along	answer	ask
after	always	any	ate
again	am	are	away
air	an	area	

A

be	begin	big	both
because	being	birds	brown
become	below	black	but
been	best	blue	buy
before	better	body	by
began	between	book	

B

C

call	children	color	cut
came	city	come	
car	close	could	
carry	cold	country	

C

D

did	do	don't	during
didn't	does	door	
different	doesn't	down	

D

early	eat	ever
earth	enough	every
easy	even	eye

_____   _____   _____

_____   _____   _____

_____   _____   _____

_____   _____   _____

_____   _____   _____

_____   _____   _____

_____   _____   _____

_____   _____   _____

_____   _____   _____

_____   _____   _____

_____   _____   _____

_____   _____   _____

F

family	few	food	from
far	find	for	funny
fast	first	found	
father	five	four	
feet	fly	friends	

G

gave	give	good	grow
get	giving	green	
girl	goes	group	

H

had	head	hers	hours
hand	hear	high	house
happened	heard	him	how
hard	help	his	however
has	her	home	
have	here	horse	

H

_____   _____   _____

_____   _____   _____

_____   _____   _____

_____   _____   _____

_____   _____   _____

_____   _____   _____

_____   _____   _____

_____   _____   _____

_____   _____   _____

_____   _____   _____

_____   _____   _____

_____   _____   _____

_____   _____   _____

idea   into   its

important   it's

J, K

jump	keep	knew
just	kind	know

J, K

last	left	light	live
later	let	like	look
learn	letter	list	low
leave	life	little	

made	mark	miss	move
make	may	mother	music
many	might	mountain	must

M

N

near	never	next	not
need	new	night	now

of	once	order	own
off	one	our	
old	open	out	
on	or	over	

page	piece	please	pull
paper	plant	point	put
picture	play	pretty	

P, Q

R

ran	really	ride	room
reached	red	right	round
read	remember	river	run

R

_____   _____   _____

_____   _____   _____

_____   _____   _____

_____   _____   _____

_____   _____   _____

_____   _____   _____

_____   _____   _____

_____   _____   _____

_____   _____   _____

_____   _____   _____

_____   _____   _____

_____   _____   _____

_____   _____   _____

said	she	so	still
saw	ship	some	stop
say	short	something	story
school	side	sometimes	such
sea	since	song	sure
second	sing	soon	
see	sit	stand	
seem	sleep	start	

S

take	then	those	too
talk	there	thought	took
tell	these	three	top
thank	they	to	tree
that	they're	today	try
their	think	together	turn
them	this	told	two

T

U, V

| under | upon | use | very |
| until | us | usually | |

W

walk	went	white	without
want	were	who	work
was	what	whole	world
wash	when	why	would
watch	where	will	write
waves	which	wish	
well	while	with	

yellow   you   your

yes   young

X,Y,Z